Discovering SELF:

"Who Am I?"
(Book One)

Discovering SELF:

"Who Am I?"
(Book One)

by

Dr. Antwion M. Yowe

Sunday School Publishing Board
Nashville, Tennessee

For information, address Townsend Press:
330 Charlotte Avenue, Nashville, Tennessee 37201-1188

ISBN: 978-1-939225-25-2

Contents

Foreword

Discovering SELF: "Who Am I?" (Book One) is the first in a series of much-needed dialogue between congregants and their quest for biblical and theological meaning. Too much of what occurs in today's society is based on misinformation and the lack of humility to make necessary and timely changes to set the record straight in individual situations.

The time has come for people of God to stop seeking self-help books and getting inappropriate advice and counsel from persons who are not equipped to expound on the Word of God. When God's people actually take the time to study to show themselves approved, they will discover that God really does use the simple things in life to confound the wise. *Discovering SELF: "Who Am I?"* is a book that helps the reader understand the complexities of *self* from both the biblical and social perspectives.

Readers will walk away from this book affirmed, energized, and transformed. They will give this book to friends and they will share it with their pastor as a Christian education resource. If you are hungry for a word from the Lord in a user-friendly, easy-to-read, easy-to-understand-and-apply format, then *"Who Am I?"* and the entire series are just what the *doctor ordered.*

Dr. Donnell J. Moore
Church Physicians Consulting

Chapter Summary

Discovering SELF—
Through Seeking, Evaluating, Loving, and Finding

<u>Scriptural Theme</u>
Keep a close watch on yourself and on the teaching. Persist in this, for by so doing you will save both yourself and your hearers.—1 Timothy 4:16 (ESV)

Bible Study Quarter One Overview:

Chapter 1: The Danger of Not Knowing Who You Are
In our biblical case study, we will study the experience of four young men who exhibited a remarkable sense of self amid challenge and conflict. We will see how having a strong sense of identity enabled them to make wise life decisions that led to success, in spite of the odds that were against them.

Chapter 2: Staying True to You
In this week's biblical case study, our subject is one that did not fit the mold of Jewish society. His true identity did not conform to the perception of his peers. As we examine the text, we will take notice of how the subject responded to the challenge of remaining true to himself.

Chapter 3: Identity in Crisis (Part 1)
Our biblical case study is found in Mark 5:1-20. As we take a closer look at this passage, we will observe a man who had found himself in a perilous position. He was in grave danger because he had lost his identity.

Chapter 4: Identity in Crisis (Part 2)
In seeking to develop our identities, it is natural to define our "selves" by belonging to someone or a group. Everyone needs a

friend. Sometimes, in the case of adolescents (but to some measure adults also), the need for friendship can generate a desperate desire to gain validation from others— no matter the cost. As the biblical case study in this chapter will illustrate, not all *friends* or associates have our best interests at heart.

Chapter 5: In the Beginning
In this week's study, we will examine the creation of the first man. We will also contemplate how the knowledge of the first man translates into a better understanding of who we are and how we should be defined.

Chapter 6: Pushing Back when God Is Pushing You Forward
In our passage for this chapter, we will discuss the nation of Israel's being led out of Egypt. Israel had been hand-picked to be God's special people; therefore, there should have been no question as to their identity. The Lord proved that He set them apart for something sacred when He protected them from the plagues of Egypt. There were no doubts about who the Israelites were when they marched through the Red Sea on dry land, while Pharaoh's army was swallowed by its unrelenting waters. Having witnessed these miracles, one would suppose that each Israelite should have had a very clear sense of identity.

Chapter 7: The Truth about Me
This chapter's biblical case study offers an intimate glimpse into the life of King David of Israel. David was known as a man of courage, honor, wisdom, and loyalty. Yet, David was only a man, and as such, he suffered flaws of character. As we will see, David was not always immediately honest with himself regarding his own character weaknesses.

Chapter 8: The ABCs of Discovering Ourselves
This chapter's case study we will look at the life of the apostle Peter. Peter was a zealous follower of Christ but he possessed some serious character flaws. Peter thought that he knew all there was to know about his character and identity. He was sure that he would be

the most faithful of the Lord's disciples. However, Peter overlooked a few things. Only after following the *ABCs of self-discovery* was he able to become the man that he and the Lord wanted him to be.

Chapter 9: The Journey (Part 1)—Spiritual Autobiography

The purpose of this chapter is to help us to see the importance of composing our own spiritual autobiographies in order to better understand our unique identities. Our biblical case study is none other than Saul the Pharisee, who underwent a conversion experience after an encounter with the Lord. God changed his name to Paul and later Paul became an apostle. In following Paul's journey through conversion, we will observe how his experiences affected the man that he would become.

Chapter 10: The Journey (Part 2)—Context

In this chapter, the apostle Paul's journey will teach us how he applied knowledge of his context to enable him to be a well-rounded minister of the Lord. Throughout the course of his ministerial career, Paul found himself in various contexts that differed greatly from one another. Paul employed the use of keen observation and research to gain a deeper understanding of his environment, as we will note in this chapter's biblical case study.

Chapter 11: The Journey (Part 3)—Synergy

Continuing with Paul's ministry, we note that God placed Paul in various contexts; as he adapted to the various settings, Paul became a better minister. His ministry growth enabled him to accomplish the Lord's plan of establishing the early churches. Both Paul and the context mutually benefited from Paul's spiritual growth and maturity.

Chapter 12: "Who Am I?"

King David penned a heart-stirring psalm in order to express his appreciation for the unique identity he possessed and the relationship that he shared with the Lord. By reflecting on this psalm, we are reminded that despite our faults, we are beautiful in the eyes of God.

Introduction

Dear Reader,

This publication is the first in a four-part series wherein the reader's focus will be directed toward discovering and developing self. Part One of the *Discovering SELF* series is entitled *"Who Am I?"* and is followed by Part Two, *"How Do I Develop Me?"* Part Three continues with *Replacing Old Habits,* and the series concludes with Part Four, which is titled, *Living as the New You.*

This series has been designed in workbook format to encourage readers to meditate on the Word of God introspectively in order to discover and develop their true identities as believers. In this portion of the series, each chapter is patterned in a similar format. Each chapter contains a Bible passage and is followed by a study that examines the passage and assists the reader in translating the message into his or her own life. The chapters conclude with a section entitled "The Word in Action." This section prompts readers to think critically and reflectively and to record their thoughts and truths in the space provided. It is the author's sincere hope that each reader will read, apply, and uncover precious gems that will enhance their spiritual journey. In doing so, the reader will be heeding the Word's exhortation: "Keep a close watch on yourself and on the teaching. Persist in this, for by so doing you will save both yourself and your hearers" (1 Timothy 4:16, ESV).

CHAPTER 1

THE DANGER OF NOT KNOWING WHO YOU ARE

Who are you? How do you identify yourself? These are more than superficial questions. I am not asking for your name or an identification card bearing a photograph and your vital statistics. But really, who *are* you?

The psychological definition of the word *identity* is "having awareness or a keen sense of self."

- What are your characteristics—flaws and all?
- What are your strengths and weaknesses?
- What are your morals and convictions?
- What are your dreams and goals?

Being able to successfully answer the above questions will lead to your being successful in defining who you really are.

In our biblical case study, we will study the experience of four young men who exhibited a remarkable sense of self amid challenge and conflict. We will see how a strong sense of identity enabled these four men to make wise life decisions, leading to success in spite of the odds that were against them.

❖ THE PASSAGE

Daniel 1:3-20

3 Then the king ordered Ashpenaz, chief of his court officials, to bring in some of the Israelites from the royal family and the nobility—

4 young men without any physical defect, handsome, showing aptitude for every kind of learning, well informed, quick to understand, and qualified to serve in the king's palace. He was to teach them the language and literature of the Babylonians.

5 The king assigned them a daily amount of food and wine from the king's table. They were to be trained for three years, and after that they were to enter the king's service.

6 Among these were some from Judah: Daniel, Hananiah, Mishael and Azariah.

7 The chief official gave them new names: to Daniel, the name Belteshazzar; to Hananiah, Shadrach; to Mishael, Meshach; and to Azariah, Abednego.

8 But Daniel resolved not to defile himself with the royal food and wine, and he asked the chief official for permission not to defile himself this way.

9 Now God had caused the official to show favor and sympathy to Daniel,

10 but the official told Daniel, "I am afraid of my lord the king, who has assigned your food and drink. Why should he see you looking worse than the other young men your age? The king would then have my head because of you."

11 Daniel then said to the guard whom the chief official had appointed over Daniel, Hananiah, Mishael and Azariah,

12 "Please test your servants for ten days: Give us nothing but vegetables to eat and water to drink.

13 Then compare our appearance with that of the young men who eat the royal food, and treat your servants in accordance with what you see."

14 So he agreed to this and tested them for ten days.

15 At the end of the ten days they looked healthier and better nourished than any of the young men who ate the royal food.

16 So the guard took away their choice food and the wine they were to drink and gave them vegetables instead.

17 To these four young men God gave knowledge and understanding of all kinds of literature and learning. And Daniel could understand visions and dreams of all kinds.

18 At the end of the time set by the king to bring them in, the chief official presented them to Nebuchadnezzar.

19 The king talked with them, and he found none equal to Daniel, Hananiah, Mishael and Azariah; so they entered the king's service.

20 In every matter of wisdom and understanding about which the king questioned them, he found them ten times better than all the magicians and enchanters in his whole kingdom.

❖ THE STUDY

History indicates that Babylonian palaces were revered places of grandeur, filled with opulent treasures, beautiful gardens, and lavish furnishings. It is here that our four young Hebrew subjects found themselves after being torn from familiar surroundings, families, and friends. Although the passage does not indicate their exact ages, it is likely that the men were still very young, possibly teenagers. Miles away from home and all that they knew, how well would the Hebrew boys fare in their new environment? Would they assimilate into the Babylonian culture or would they develop and maintain their own individual sense of identity?

Having been raised by their Hebrew parents according to Israelite custom, the boys had been instructed from infancy in Jewish culture and taught the Law of Moses. Their parents selected for them meaningful names, strongly tied to their religious faith. As these young men grew, their upbringing shaped their morals, principles, and values. They developed unique characteristics and manifested individual strengths. In fact, the reason they were selected by the king's men was because they showed remarkable aptitude and possessed other impressive qualities.

These young men were brought to Babylon, the center of rising political power at that time, at the request of the king. For three years, they were force-fed Babylonian culture and practices. They were assigned foods that were foreign and quite offensive to their Hebrew nature. And as if that were not enough, the Babylonians changed their birth-given Hebrew names to Babylonian names with pagan connotations. All of this appears to have been an insidious scheme to make them forget their Israelite customs and practices and eradicate all vestiges of their Hebrew existence.

If this was indeed the intention of the Babylonian officials, they failed miserably. From the passage, it is quite clear that the four Hebrew boys had a strong sense of identity. Throughout the scope of this account, the writer, Daniel, continued to refer to himself and his three companions by their Hebrew names. Not only that, but it is clear that Daniel, Hananiah, Mishael, and Azariah stuck to their principles. Rather than indulging in the king's delicacies, they chose humble meals consisting of vegetables and water to maintain their personal morals and values.

We can conclude from this biblical case study that the four Hebrew boys really *knew* who they were. They possessed clearly defined identities and refused to allow imposed assimilation strategies to conform them to their new environment. Having a strong sense of self enabled the four Hebrew boys to have success and blessings. The king was impressed by their knowledge and appearance. He considered them to be more valuable than his entourage of magicians and wise men. As such, he awarded them with positions of import within his kingdom.

When we reflect on our lives, we often find a moment of clarity where we understand who we are, where we are from, and where we are going. These ideas have been shaped by our knowledge and experience. However, as the world or environment around us continually changes, if our sense of identity is weak or vague, then we may very easily find ourselves being overtaken by popular opinion, current fads, or dominating trends.

It is important that we fight to find and maintain our sense of identity. We must remember that we are all uniquely talented. If we fail to let our identities shine—if we mask them by being transformed to mirror our environment—we rob others and ourselves of our real potential. If Daniel and his friends had simply "gone along with the program," the king may have never realized their unique worth.

By establishing who we *really* are, we are laying the foundation for our personal success. This means taking more than a superficial glance or making a list of our favorable qualities. It involves an honest self-appraisal, answering the questions listed at the outset of this lesson. And it is important to remember that there is no right or wrong answer to our personal assessment. We are who we are, plain and simple. That is not to say that everything we find will be admirable or desirable, but by being candid, we can more accurately see ourselves and understand the path that is meant for us as individuals.

❖ THE WORD IN ACTION

A good name is more desirable than riches; to be esteemed is better than silver or gold.—Proverbs 22:1

1. Identify at least three people you know who use *nicknames*. Is there a meaning attached to the nickname? If so, what is it?

   _____
   _____
   _____
   _____
   _____
   _____
   _____

2. Do you think it is important that people use their given name instead of assumed names? Explain.

   _____
   _____
   _____
   _____
   _____
   _____
   _____

3. Practice referring to people by their birth name during this week, particularly those who use a nickname or an assumed name. Record their reactions.

   _____
   _____
   _____
   _____
   _____
   _____
   _____
   _____

CHAPTER **2**

STAYING TRUE TO YOU

Having a clear sense of self is only part of the battle. Maintaining our identities with a measure of consistency is equally challenging. There are many factors that may coerce us into altering or masking our true identities, but peer pressure has often been cited at the top of that list. We tend to place a very high value on how we are perceived by others. To be accepted, we may find ourselves conforming to fit into molds dictated by society. In doing so, we may find that our clear sense of identity becomes blurred.

In this week's biblical case study, our subject is one that did not fit the mold of Jewish society. His true identity did not conform to the perception of his peers. As we examine the text, we will take notice of how the subject responded to the challenge of remaining true to himself.

❖ THE PASSAGE

John 10:22-42

22 Then came the Feast of Dedication at Jerusalem. It was winter,

23 and Jesus was in the temple area walking in Solomon's Colonnade.

24 The Jews gathered around him, saying, "How long will you keep us in suspense? If you are the Christ, tell us plainly."

25 Jesus answered, "I did tell you, but you do not believe. The miracles I do in my Father's name speak for me,

26 but you do not believe because you are not my sheep.

27 My sheep listen to my voice; I know them, and they follow me.

28 I give them eternal life, and they shall never perish; no one can snatch them out of my hand.

29 My Father, who has given them to me, is greater than all; no one can snatch them out of my Father's hand.

30 I and the Father are one."

31 Again the Jews picked up stones to stone him,

32 but Jesus said to them, "I have shown you many great miracles from the Father. For which of these do you stone me?

33 "We are not stoning you for any of these," replied the Jews, "but for blasphemy, because you, a mere man, claim to be God."

34 Jesus answered them, "Is it not written in your Law, 'I have said you are gods'?

35 If he called them 'gods,' to whom the word of God came—and the Scripture cannot be broken—

36 what about the one whom the Father set apart as his very own and sent into the world? Why then do you accuse me of blasphemy because I said, 'I am God's Son'?

37 Do not believe me unless I do what my Father does.

38 But if I do it, even though you do not believe me, believe the miracles, that you may know and understand that the Father is in me, and I in the Father."

39 Again they tried to seize him, but he escaped their grasp.

40 Then Jesus went back across the Jordan to the place where John had been baptizing in the early days. Here he stayed

41 and many people came to him. They said, "Though John never performed a miraculous sign, all that John said about this man was true."

42 And in that place many believed in Jesus.

❖ THE STUDY

By now you likely have realized that our subject of study for this chapter is Jesus Himself. In this passage, we find Jesus faced with a daunting crowd bent on proving that He was not who He said He was. Their sarcasm and disbelief eventually escalated to physical intimidation. Had Jesus cowered under their coercion, He very likely could have suffered an identity crisis.

Similarly for us, one of the great challenges to our sense of identity is pressure from those who doubt our genuineness or our sincerity. We find it discouraging when, despite our efforts to remain true to our real character, others continue to make disparaging comments.

How do you respond? Are you intimidated? Do you feel the need to justify or explain yourself? Do you allow the views of others to alter your self-perception?

Of course, we know that Jesus successfully met this challenge and overcame the doubts of naysayers by remaining true to Himself and His role. By taking a closer look at this passage, we will isolate key elements that helped Jesus to avoid undergoing an identity crisis.

First, Jesus accepted the fact that not everyone would be a believer. In spite of the ample evidence presented to them, there were some who just refused to receive it. Likewise, we must understand that there will always be doubters around in the realms of our lives. However, our lifestyles and behavior provide accurate evidence that we are who we profess to be; we should not be overly concerned with the misconceptions of others.

Jesus was willing to let His "actions speak louder than words." The miracles He performed gave what should have been unquestionable authentication to His identity. In a similar way, our actions speak louder than any argument that we could ever present on our behalf.

Even when those stubborn Jews refused to believe, Jesus was not discouraged because He knew that those who really mattered would accept His identity. Jesus said that His *sheep* would know Him, and because of their loyalty, He would keep them close, and no one would be able to break that bond. This is an important realization. Those who matter will accept our identities. Once we weed out the fickle and fake, and determine those who are truly in our corner, the opinions of those outside our circle will no longer weigh heavily on our minds.

It is also noteworthy that Jesus was not intimidated by the abrasiveness of the nonbelieving Jews. Jesus understood this fact: those unbelievers stood condemned in the face of Jesus' genuineness. Because they were not truthful regarding their own identities, they did not want to accept the genuineness of Jesus. When we allow our individuality to shine, those who repress their own identities for whatever reason are threatened and feel as though our genuineness is making them look bad. Thus, they retaliate through intimidating speech and character attacks. Like Jesus, we must recognize the situation for what it is and refuse to allow frauds to alter our personal perception of our identities.

It is also interesting that those who were present deliberately chose to remain ignorant, despite Jesus' irrefutable logic. This goes to show that such individuals are not worthy of any explanation or justification because they purposely bury their heads in the sand. The younger generation has bestowed a term to label those who desperately seek to tear others down: *haters*. These persons are called haters because they dislike the fact that others are genuine, they hate the fact that others are confident in their identities, and they hate the fact that others' confidence is leading them to success. Understand that haters are going to hate. It is their job. However, we can successfully avoid an identity crisis by not cowering to their intimidation, but remaining true to ourselves.

❖ THE WORD IN ACTION

Anyone who listens to the word but does not do what it says is like a man who looks at his face in a mirror and, after looking at himself, goes away and immediately forgets what he looks like.
—James 1:23-24

Your beauty should not come from outward adornment, such as braided hair and the wearing of gold jewelry and fine clothes. Instead, it should be that of your inner self, the unfading beauty of a gentle and quiet spirit, which is of great worth in God's sight.
—1 Peter 3:3-4

Each day this week, take ten minutes to look at your reflection in a mirror. As you look into the mirror, focus on some trait or characteristic that makes you who you are. Try to dig beyond the surface of mere appearance and, using your journal pages provided, write about what you see.

Day One

_____
_____
_____
_____
_____
_____

Day Two

_____
_____
_____
_____
_____
_____

Day Three

_____
_____
_____
_____
_____
_____

Day Four

_____
_____
_____
_____
_____
_____

Day Five

_____

_____

_____

_____

_____

_____

Day Six

_____

_____

_____

_____

_____

Day Seven

_____

_____

_____

_____

_____

_____

CHAPTER 3

IDENTITY IN CRISIS

(Part 1)

We sometimes have the tendency to view ourselves through rose-colored glasses. We justify or hide our faults. We play up our admirable traits. Few take the time to seriously contemplate who they really are. Quite frankly, some of us are afraid to dig deeper than the surface because we are afraid of what we may find. Still, ignorance is not bliss. A lack of self-knowledge translates into unused potential, troubled relationships, and discontented lives.

Our biblical case study is found in Mark 5:1-20. As we take a closer look at this account, we will observe a man who had found himself in a perilous position. He was in grave danger because he had lost his identity.

❖ THE PASSAGE

Mark 5:1-20

1 They went across the lake to the region of the Gerasenes.

2 When Jesus got out of the boat, a man with an evil spirit came from the tombs to meet him.

3 This man lived in the tombs, and no one could bind him any more, not even with a chain.

4 For he had often been chained hand and foot, but he tore the chains apart and broke the irons on his feet. No one was strong enough to subdue him.

5 Night and day among the tombs and in the hills he would cry out and cut himself with stones.

6 When he saw Jesus from a distance, he ran and fell on his knees in front of him.

7 He shouted at the top of his voice, "What do you want with me, Jesus, Son of the Most High God? Swear to God that you won't torture me!"

8 For Jesus had said to him, "Come out of this man, you evil spirit!"

9 Then Jesus asked him, "What is your name?" "My name is Legion," he replied, "for we are many."

10 And he begged Jesus again and again not to send them out of the area.

11 A large herd of pigs was feeding on the nearby hillside.

12 The demons begged Jesus, "Send us among the pigs; allow us to go into them."

13 He gave them permission, and the evil spirits came out and went into the pigs. The herd, about two thousand in number, rushed down the steep bank into the lake and were drowned.

14 Those tending the pigs ran off and reported this in the town and countryside, and the people went out to see what had happened.

15 When they came to Jesus, they saw the man who had been possessed by the legion of demons, sitting there, dressed and in his right mind; and they were afraid.

16 Those who had seen it told the people what had happened to the demon-possessed man—and told about the pigs as well.

17 Then the people began to plead with Jesus to leave their region.

18 As Jesus was getting into the boat, the man who had been demon-possessed begged to go with him.

19 Jesus did not let him, but said, "Go home to your family and tell them how much the Lord has done for you, and how he has had mercy on you."

20 So the man went away and began to tell in the Decapolis how much Jesus had done for him. And all the people were amazed."

❖ THE STUDY

This poor man had suffered an extreme case of identity crisis. Evil and unclean spirits were repressing his real identity. It is ironic that the gospel writer named only the multiple personalities existing inside of him and not the man himself.

Yet, despite the war going on within him, this man from the Gerasenes had enough consciousness to know that he was in need of help. *He* approached the Lord. The real man struggled to emerge by reaching out to Jesus. If we find ourselves on the dangerous edge of losing our sense of self, we should remember that God is able to help us maintain or even retrieve, if necessary, our inner stability.

It is unfortunate that life often leads us to *wear many faces*. For the sake of professionalism, we may develop a business persona. For personal or social reasons, we may mask who we really are. In the face of adversity, we develop an alter ego. For the pretense of love, we may adopt a personality completely foreign to our own. Author Nathaniel Hawthorne observed, "No man, for any considerable period, can wear one face to himself and another to a multitude without finally getting bewildered as to which may be true."

While some adaptations are necessary and justifiable, we must recognize the real danger of losing ourselves entirely. When we consistently repress who we truly are, like the Gerasenes man, we risk being overtaken by impulsive behavior that may result in harm to others and ourselves. Because of his erratic and even violent tendencies manifested by the spirits invading his body, this man found himself isolated from the world and those he loved. Likewise, when we submerge ourselves in pseudo-personalities, we segregate ourselves from the possibility of developing meaningful relationships.

Lack of self-awareness is the first stop on the path to self-destruction. In the account, Legion so thoroughly occupied the man that he neither realized the threat that he posed to others nor the damage that he inflicted upon himself. Similarly, we threaten the happiness and trust of those around us when we deceive them with our false identities. Not only that, but when we indulge in self-deception by neglecting to understand who we really are, we set ourselves up for failure. Our lives become a cesspool of wasted potential. Next stop: loss of self-worth.

Self-worth, simply put, is our sense of personal value. In our case study, the man from the Gerasenes was so consumed by his alter ego that he began to lose his sense of worth. He chose not to identify himself by his Christian name, but by the name *Legion* instead. Even when the Lord called out to the man to grant him release, he begged the Lord not to send the spirits away. The spirits had insidiously depreciated the man's self-worth in his own mind to the point that he felt he could not exist in their absence. In fact, so overtaken by his multiple personalities, the man forgot that he was first and foremost a child of God.

When we endeavor to perpetrate artificial personas, we risk losing not only our true selves, but also our true value. The pretenses that we display to fool the world eventually deceive us into believing that we are worthless—nothing more than hollow mannequins beneath the masks we wear. We may have forgotten that we, too, are first and foremost children of God. That fact alone gives us value beyond comprehension—for to be a child of God is priceless.

Like the Gerasenes man, we may be dangerously close to losing our real identities to the depths of oblivion. In fact, this man was very possibly on the brink of self-destruction. Yet, somewhere in his subconscious, the man reached out to the Lord and the Lord saw through to the soul and heart of the *real* man. Jesus has the ability to see one for who he or she really is. Hebrews 4:13 reads, "Nothing in all creation is hidden from God's sight. Everything is uncovered and laid bare before the eyes of him to whom we must give account."

Jesus was able to find value worthy of redemption in this man's life and, in His mercy, helped this man to regain his balance—to retrieve his true identity. The Lord is doing the same thing for us. He is looking for His children who have lost themselves. He is searching for those of us who have forgotten who we really are. He will help us to reclaim our identities and appreciate our real worth.

Now, let's imagine what would have happened if Jesus had not rescued this man who was masked by Legion. The text tells us that almost immediately after Jesus sent the spirits into the swine, the pigs dove into a lake and drowned. This tragic end likely would have been the fate of the Gerasenes man. Completely consumed by his alter ego, and unable to control their manic thoughts and actions, the man probably would have committed irreversible harm to himself.

It is reasonable to believe that the Gerasenes man had languished for years with this internal war. Over the course of time he lost everything—his home, his family, his friends, his livelihood, and his purpose. Had Jesus not saved this man from himself, he would never have had the opportunity to gain any of these things back. Yet, as we read the text, we learn that the man regained his senses, recovered his dignity, and was dispatched to his family. He gained a new sense of purpose as he went back to his hometown to tell everyone about what the Lord had done for him.

If we have found that we are in danger of losing our true identities, then our reflecting on this passage should help us to appreciate the perilous condition that we are in. We risk severing treasured relationships, losing our sense of worth, wasting our true potential, and neglecting our holy purpose. However, this text also helps us to remember that as long as we have life in our bodies, we are never beyond the loving reach of Jesus. He is always there, seeing through to the real person buried beneath the masks that we have put on. We have only but to approach Him, reach out to Him like the man from the Gerasenes, and He will help us peel back the layers so that our true identities can shine through.

❖ THE WORD IN ACTION

My soul finds rest in God alone; my salvation comes from him. He alone is my rock and my salvation; he is my fortress, I will never be shaken. How long will you assault a man? Would all of you throw him down—this leaning wall, this tottering fence? They fully intend to topple him from his lofty place; they take delight in lies. With their mouths they bless, but in their hearts they curse.—Psalm 62:1-4

1. Recall a situation in which your genuineness or sincerity was questioned. How did you feel? Did you try to justify or explain your case? Why or why not?

   _____

   _____

   _____

_____

_____

_____

_____

_____

_____

_____

2. Do you feel your lifestyle and behavior *always* accurately represents who you really are on the inside? Explain.

_____

_____

_____

_____

_____

_____

_____

_____

_____

3. Think about some of the people around the perimeter of your life who challenge your identity. Who are they? Are they relevant? If they are, are any of their points valid? If they are not, are you willing to remove them from your circle? What can you do to alter their misconception?

_____

_____

_____

_____

_____

_____

_____

_____

CHAPTER 4

IDENTITY IN CRISIS

(Part 2)

Erik Erikson theorized that one's identity is primarily forged during the adolescent years. According to Erikson, adolescents work through a phase where they try out different roles and perhaps present different *selves* in different situations. The optimal results are that that young individual will eventually resolve his/her role confusion by reshaping his/her self-definition to unite the various roles into one stable, consistent personality or identity (Erikson, 1963). However, most people battle with the age-old question of "Who am I?" well past their teenage years and revisit it at key turning points in their adult lives. In instances where an individual has achieved a clear sense of self, that identity is vulnerable to situations and circumstances.

In our seeking to develop our identities, it is natural to define our identification in part by belonging to someone or a group. Everyone needs friends. Sometimes, especially in the case of adolescents (but to some measure, adults also), the need for friendship can generate a desperate desire to gain validation from others—no matter the cost. As the biblical case study in this chapter will illustrate, not all friends or associates have our best interests at heart.

❖ THE PASSAGE

Judges 16:4-21

4 Some time later, he fell in love with a woman in the Valley of Sorek whose name was Delilah.

5 The rulers of the Philistines went to her and said, "See if you can lure him into showing you the secret of his great strength and how we can overpower him so we may tie him up and subdue him. Each one of us will give you eleven hundred shekels of silver."

6 So Delilah said to Samson, "Tell me the secret of your great strength and how you can be tied up and subdued."

7 Samson answered her, "If anyone ties me with seven fresh thongs that have not been dried, I'll become as weak as any other man."

8 Then the rulers of the Philistines brought her seven fresh thongs that had not been dried, and she tied him with them.

9 With the men hidden in the room, she called to him, "Samson, the Philistines are upon you!" But he snapped the thongs easily as a piece of string snaps when it comes close to a flame. So the secret of his strength was not discovered.

10 Then Delilah said to Samson, "You have made a fool of me; you lied to me. Come now, tell me how you can be tied."

11 He said, "If anyone ties me securely with new ropes that have never been used, I'll become as weak as any other man."

12 So Delilah took new ropes and tied him with them. Then, with the men hidden in the room, she called to him, "Samson, the Philistines are upon you!" But he snapped the ropes off his arms as if they were threads.

13 Delilah then said to Samson, "Until now, you have been making a fool of me and lying to me. Tell me how you can be tied." He replied, "If you weave the seven braids of my head into the fabric [on the loom] and tighten it with the pin, I'll become as weak as any other man." So while he was sleeping, Delilah took the seven braids of his head, wove them into the fabric

14 and tightened it with the pin. Again she called to him, "Samson, the Philistines are upon you!" He awoke from his sleep and pulled up the pin and the loom, with the fabric.

15 Then she said to him, "How can you say, 'I love you,' when you won't confide in me? This is the third time you have made a fool of me and haven't told me the secret of your great strength."

16 With such nagging she prodded him day after day until he was tired to death.

17 So he told her everything. "No razor has ever been used on my head," he said, "because I have been a Nazirite set apart to God since birth. If my head were shaved, my strength would leave me, and I would become as weak as any other man."

18 When Delilah saw that he had told her everything, she sent word to the rulers of the Philistines, "Come back once more; he has told me everything." So the rulers of the Philistines returned with the silver in their hands.

19 Having put him to sleep on her lap, she called a man to shave off the seven braids of his hair, and so began to subdue him. And his strength left him.

20 Then she called, "Samson, the Philistines are upon you!" He awoke from his sleep and thought, "I'll go out as before and shake myself free." But he did not know that the LORD had left him.

21 Then the Philistines seized him, gouged out his eyes and took him down to Gaza. Binding him with bronze shackles, they set him to grinding in the prison.

❖ THE STUDY

Before we delve into this passage, let us first establish some background on our subject. Samson's birth was the result of one of the few miraculous conceptions recorded in the Bible. An angel appeared to the sterile wife of Manoah and announced that she would give birth to a son. With this announcement, the angel went on to identify who this child would be. There were three key elements to Samson's identity:

1. From the time of his birth until his death, he would be a Nazirite set aside for special service to God.
2. He would initiate Israel's deliverance from their forty-year oppression under the Philistines.
3. No razor was to be used to cut his hair.

So even before Samson was born, his identity had been established for him. His parents sought to raise him in accord with the instructions of the angel, and so it is reasonable to conclude that Samson had a very clear sense of who he was and his purpose.

Moving forward to the scene of our passage, we find Samson as an adult who has fallen deeply in love. Love is often a positive emotion and if properly cultivated, it should enhance who we are. However, in Samson's case, it is apparent that his love became obsessive and caused him to lose focus.

Samson, who incidentally had been betrayed by his first wife (who was also a Philistine), became enraptured by Delilah, but Delilah had secretly made a pact with the Philistine men. Reading the passage, we find that three times Delilah tried to trap Samson and deliver him over to them. Now if Samson had been thinking rationally—had he maintained a clear sense of who he was—he should have immediately recognized what was happening. From birth, he had been taught that he would begin Israel's deliverance from the Philistines. The Israelites and Philistines were sworn enemies! It should not have been difficult for Samson to realize what was at play. Unfortunately, Samson had become absorbed in his relationship with Delilah and forgot the importance of maintaining his own identity.

Similarly today, we may allow ourselves to become absorbed in an obsessive love. It may not necessarily involve a romantic liaison—it could be our careers, our families, or anything that causes us to lose focus on the truth of our identities. While these things may be important, we must be careful not to lose ourselves into them completely. We cannot allow them to define who we are.

In the case of Samson, obsessive love caused him to forget what the angel had told his parents. It caused him to forget the uniqueness of his strength. It caused him to forget that the Philistines were his enemy and they were not to be trusted. Delilah continued to apply pressure. She knew that Samson was vulnerable in his love for her. Notice the tactic that she used in her final attempt to get Samson to reveal his secret. The threat of losing her was evidently too much for Samson to bear—so instead of holding on to his identity, he gave her what she wanted.

We must be on guard against obsessions that would weaken our identities. If we are not careful, we will forget our morals, values, strengths, and goals, which make us whom we really are. Stripped of these, we are vulnerable and exposed, much like Samson was without his hair. So thoroughly was Samson submerged in his passion for Delilah that he did not realize what he had done until it was too late. Robbed of his strength and God's Spirit, Samson was captured and blinded by the Philistines. It can be said that he was literally blinded by obsession.

From this biblical case study then, we see the danger in our allowing external forces to overshadow our identities. When we repress our individuality in an effort to please others, or achieve a certain position or status, we are putting our identities in crisis. Without a clear sense of who we are, we lose our strength of character. Like Samson, we become weak and vulnerable, unable to successfully meet challenges using our full potential.

❖ THE WORD IN ACTION

1. What personal potential obsessions threaten to obscure your identity?

    _____

    _____

    _____

    _____

    _____

2. Having identified potential threats that may weaken your sense of self, what proactive measures are you willing to take to circumvent them?

    _____

    _____

    _____

    _____

    _____

    _____

CHAPTER 5

IN THE BEGINNING

It has been argued that we are products of our environments. To some extent this may be true, but it is only because we have allowed this to be so. Romans 12:2 implies that we have the power to escape the identities forced upon us by society. Here, the apostle Paul encouraged believers: "Do not conform any longer to the pattern of this world, but be transformed by the renewing of your mind. Then you will be able to test and approve what God's will is—his good, pleasing and perfect will."

In other words, we do not have to be products of our environments but we can be the people that God desires us to be by renewing our minds by the power of His Word.

We must recognize that we were not meant to be simply products of our environments, but we are the creation of God's own hands. To understand who we are, we must first understand our beginning. The book of Genesis contains the record of creation, including that of humans.

In this week's study, we will examine the creation of the first man and contemplate how this knowledge translates into a better understanding of who we are and what should define us.

❖ THE PASSAGES

Genesis 1:21-27

21 So God created the great creatures of the sea and every living and moving thing with which the water teems, according to their kinds, and every winged bird according to its kind. And God saw that it was good.

22 God blessed them and said, "Be fruitful and increase in number and fill the water in the seas, and let the birds increase on the earth."

23 And there was evening, and there was morning— the fifth day.

24 And God said, "Let the land produce living creatures according to their kinds: livestock, creatures that move along the ground, and wild animals, each according to its kind." And it was so.

25 God made the wild animals according to their kinds, the livestock according to their kinds, and all the creatures that move along the ground according to their kinds. And God saw that it was good.

26 Then God said, "Let us make man in our image, in our likeness, and let them rule over the fish of the sea and the birds of the air, over the livestock, over all the earth, and over all the creatures that move along the ground."

27 So God created man in his own image, in the image of God he created him; male and female he created them.

Genesis 2:7

7 the LORD God formed the man from the dust of the ground and breathed into his nostrils the breath of life, and the man became a living being.

❖ THE STUDY

Humans are unique among all of God's creations. While God created all living creatures and assigned them to earthly domains, animals were created according to their *own* kind. Animals have natural instinct and lack spiritual characteristics. Humans, on the other hand, were created to be individuals made in God's image.

What does that really mean—that we are made in God's image? Unlike animals, God has given humanity moral capacity. We have the ability to assimilate knowledge, to reason, and to make decisions based on our own self-awareness. The Lord has endowed us with His godly characteristics, such as love, fairness, mercy, patience, and kindness.

Of course, we know that this image was tarnished by the sin of the first man and woman—Adam and Eve. As a result of the introduction of sin to the human race, imperfection has birthed numerous character flaws. Second Timothy 3:1-7 identifies behaviors that would characterize those who allow worldly influence to shape their identities:
- Lovers of themselves, pleasures, and money
- Boastful and proud
- Abusive and disobedient
- Ungrateful and unforgiving
- Slanderous and unholy

These verses also mention that individuals would have a *form of godliness*, and rightly so, because remember, in the beginning we were *all* created in God's image. Sadly, though, some will undergo such a drastic transformation that their godliness will be barely recognizable. According to the Scripture, they are forever learning but "never able to acknowledge the truth." Is it because the knowledge that they feed their minds is not godly and spiritual? They busy themselves learning empty philosophies and fleeting social trends that shape their moral sense. They remain deliberately ignorant so as not to see the truth about who they really are as opposed to who God meant for them to be.

Still, we possess the potential to reject the influence of social constraints and allow God's Spirit—the same Spirit that He breathed into the first man—to enliven us to become worthy reflections of Him. That Spirit can produce in us the godly qualities cited in Galatians 5:22-23: love, joy, peace, patience, kindness, goodness, faithfulness, gentleness, and self-control. This is what God intended from the beginning. Even though we are imperfect, He is still giving us the Spirit that we need to produce identities defined by His Word.

Referring again to our passages in the book of Genesis, we discover that humans are also uniquely set apart from God's other creations—in that God has given us a purpose. God told the first human couple to produce offspring who would also be born in His image. He also gave them an assignment related to the earth and its animal inhabitants. In this, we learn that our identities should be defined by the purpose that God has spoken into our lives. You see, there is a marriage between who we are and why we are here. The two concepts merge together to complement and complete one another.

As believers, we must acknowledge that only God has the right and ability to ordain our lives with purpose. Society, politics, worldly trends, peers, and even family should not have the deciding vote in how we identify ourselves. In the beginning, it was God's Word that declared that humans should be made in His image. It was God's breath that gave life to the human body. It was God's will that humans have a purposeful life. It is, therefore, by the Word of God that we seek to define our identities according to His good purpose.

❖ THE WORD IN ACTION

1. We often feel a tremendous pressure to conform to societal influences and trends. How does this chapter encourage you personally to resist being squeezed into a personality that is ungodly?

_____

_____

_____

_____

_____

_____

_____

_____

_____

2. From what source do you feel that you receive the strongest pressure to develop a personality contrary to what God has ordained for you?

_____

_____

_____

_____

_____

_____

3. How do you resolve to overcome or resist the pressures that you may face?

_____

_____

_____

_____

_____

_____

CHAPTER **6**

PUSHING BACK WHEN GOD IS PUSHING YOU FORWARD

As we learned in the previous chapter, the Word of God should define our identities. With the gift of the Holy Spirit, we can discover the persons that we are meant to be. However, there are times when believers are resistant to the things that God introduces into our lives.

God often places wonderful things before us and lovingly prompts us to follow a course of action that will take us where we need to be. When we are unsure of ourselves, we may struggle to become that which we were never meant to be. It is an unfortunate predicament because we are in effect fighting against the Lord.

In our passage for this chapter, we discuss the nation of Israel's being led out of Egypt. Israel had been handpicked to be God's special people. There should have been no question as to their identities. The Lord had proved that He set them apart as sacred when He protected them from the plagues of Egypt. There were no doubts about who they were when they marched through the Red Sea on dry land, while Pharaoh's army was swallowed by its unrelenting waters. Having witnessed these miracles, one would suppose that each Israelite should have had a very clear sense of identity.

Sadly, though, the Israelites allowed their self-awareness to waver. They began to question who they were and what they were capable of as God's chosen people. As a result, they began to resist what God had already spoken into their lives.

❖ THE PASSAGE

Numbers 13:26-33

26 They came back to Moses and Aaron and the whole Israelite community at Kadesh in the Desert of Paran. There they reported to them and to the whole assembly and showed them the fruit of the land.

27 They gave Moses this account: "We went into the land to which you sent us, and it does flow with milk and honey! Here is its fruit.

28 But the people who live there are powerful, and the cities are fortified and very large. We even saw descendants of Anak there.

29 The Amalekites live in the Negev; the Hittites, Jebusites and Amorites live in the hill country; and the Canaanites live near the sea and along the Jordan."

30 Then Caleb silenced the people before Moses and said, "We should go up and take possession of the land, for we can certainly do it."

31 But the men who had gone up with him said, "We can't attack those people; they are stronger than we are."

32 And they spread among the Israelites a bad report about the land they had explored. They said, "The land we explored devours those living in it. All the people we saw there are of great size.

33 We saw the Nephilim there (the descendants of Anak come from the Nephilim). We seemed like grasshoppers in our own eyes, and we looked the same to them."

❖ THE STUDY

God had chosen this nation for His good purpose and He was pushing them forward to inherit bountiful blessings. Long before He rescued them from Egypt, the Lord had promised Abraham that He would bless his offspring that would become the nation of Israel with an inheritance—the Promised Land. Now, after having brought them through great adversity, the Lord was ushering the nation on into the Land of Promise.

It is the Lord who puts us in position to receive His blessings. In order to be where we need to be so that we can receive our reward, we may find ourselves amid trials and adversity. Yet, we must be conscious of the fact that what God has for us is for us. If He is pushing us forward, then He will bring us through whatever stands between our Promised Land and us.

Before they were to enter into the land, Moses was instructed to send spies ahead of the assembly of Israel. Those spies were to explore and report back what they found in the new territory. Upon their return, Moses and the Israelite nation were told of the rich and bountiful produce that was to be found there. However, they also recounted a fearsome description of the cities and their inhabitants.

Two of the spies, though, retained a clear sense of identity. They remained confident that the Promised Land was within their grasp. Caleb and Joshua knew that if God was pushing them forward into this land, then their success was guaranteed.

Unfortunately, the ten remaining spies lacked such conviction. They allowed themselves to be intimidated by the appearance of mere humans. Clearly they had forgotten who they were as a people. Had they remembered that they were the ones whom the Lord had delivered from Egypt, guided through a dry seabed, led by cloud and by fire, fed with bread and meat from heaven—had they recalled all these things, they would have known without question that they were a special people being directed with God's protection upon them.

Their having awareness of their identities would have prevented them from becoming resistant to the urgings of God. Instead, the report of the cowardly spies caused them to develop a distorted view of themselves. Though a mighty nation, they reckoned themselves to be like lowly grasshoppers in comparison to the people of the land.

This should serve well as a lesson for us today. We must be cautious of those who would dissuade us from moving forward toward what God has for us. Peer pressure and intimidation can cause us to lose sight of who we really are and what it is that we stand for. We are unable then to tap into our inner strength. Out of fear, we push backward when we should be going forward. On the other hand, if we surround ourselves with persons like Joshua and Caleb, who possessed strong conviction and a keen sense of self-awareness, then we will likewise be encouraged to keep moving in the direction that the Lord is leading us.

Because they pushed backward when God was trying to push them forward, the children of Israel were struggling against what the Lord had purposed for them. They were meant to be heirs of a great promise but instead as they pushed against that destiny, they took on a new identity not intended for them. Instead of heirs living in the land of their inheritance, they became wanderers in the great wilderness for forty long years. Not one of the Israelites who resisted God's leadership set foot in the Promised Land. They all died as nomads in the desert.

Similarly, when we work against God's will for us, we forge identities not meant for us. Take note that the Hebrew word *sa·tan'* literally means "resister." Therefore, when we resist our divine destiny we no longer manifest ourselves to be children of God. Instead, we adopt identities as spawns of Satan. As believers, we never want to be identified with that evil master. So, then, we must be ever cautious not to push backwards when the Lord is moving us forward.

❖ THE WORD IN ACTION

1. The Israelites were frightened by the appearance of the inhabitants who looked like giants. What personal giants stand between you and your destiny?

   _____

   _____

   _____

   _____

   _____

   _____

2. The Israelites showed a lack of faith because they failed to reflect on the things that God had already brought them through. Meditate on the giants that the Lord has already removed from your path. How does this give you confidence to face the future?

   _____

   _____

   _____

   _____

   _____

   _____

CHAPTER 7

THE TRUTH ABOUT ME

If we hope to improve ourselves, we must be candid about who we really are. We must take a critical look at ourselves and evaluate the good, the bad, and even the ugly. It is only by conducting an honest self-appraisal that we can claim mastery over the personality traits that are hindering us from becoming the persons that God intended us to be.

It is not an easy task to bear our own faults and personal feelings. Human nature pushes us to accentuate our strengths while minimizing or justifying our flaws. We may even purposely turn a blind eye to behaviors or actions that cast us in a less-than-favorable light. However, if we are sincere in our quest to discover and improve ourselves, then we must be open and honest about our character.

This chapter's biblical case study offers an intimate glimpse into the life of King David of Israel. David was known as a man of courage, honor, wisdom, and loyalty. Yet, David was but a man, and as such, he suffered flaws of character. As we will see, David was not always immediately honest with himself regarding his own character weaknesses.

❖ THE PASSAGE

2 Samuel 12:1-13

1 The LORD sent Nathan to David. When he came to him, he said, "There were two men in a certain town, one rich and the other poor.

2 The rich man had a very large number of sheep and cattle,

3 but the poor man had nothing except one little ewe lamb he had bought. He raised it, and it grew up with him and his children. It shared his food, drank from his cup and even slept in his arms. It was like a daughter to him.

4 Now a traveler came to the rich man, but the rich man refrained from taking one of his own sheep or cattle to prepare a meal for the traveler who had come to him. Instead, he took the ewe lamb that belonged to the poor man and prepared it for the one who had come to him."

5 David burned with anger against the man and said to Nathan, "As surely as the LORD lives, the man who did this deserves to die!

6 He must pay for that lamb four times over, because he did such a thing and had no pity."

7 Then Nathan said to David, "You are the man! This is what the LORD, the God of Israel, says: 'I anointed you king over Israel, and I delivered you from the hand of Saul.

8 I gave your master's house to you, and your master's wives into your arms. I gave you the house of Israel and Judah. And if all this had been too little, I would have given you even more.

9 Why did you despise the word of the LORD by doing what is evil in his eyes? You struck down

Uriah the Hittite with the sword and took his wife to be your own. You killed him with the sword of the Ammonites.

10 Now, therefore, the sword will never depart from your house, because you despised me and took the wife of Uriah the Hittite to be your own.'

11 This is what the LORD says: 'Out of your own household I am going to bring calamity upon you. Before your very eyes I will take your wives and give them to one who is close to you, and he will lie with your wives in broad daylight.

12 You did it in secret, but I will do this thing in broad daylight before all Israel.'"

13 Then David said to Nathan, "I have sinned against the LORD." Nathan replied, "The LORD has taken away your sin. You are not going to die."

❖ THE STUDY

Before we dissect the passage, let us first consider the events that led up to Nathan's having to deliver this message to David. David was many great things during his lifetime—a talented musician, a trustworthy shepherd, a devoted servant, a brave warrior, and a noble king. Unfortunately, David also had an Achilles's heel for beautiful women. His weakness led to covetousness. One day while walking on the roof of his palace, David observed an attractive woman bathing. Tempted by his rooftop voyeurism, David found out her identity and even though he was told that she was married, he had her brought to him. David later learned that a child had been conceived as a result of their affair. To cover the matter, David schemed to first fool the woman's husband and possibly have him think that the child was his own. When that plan failed, he sought to have the husband placed in a vulnerable position on the battlefield so that he might be killed.

A reasonable person would be appalled at David's treachery. David, however, somehow justified his actions. He went as far as to state that the death of the woman's husband was nothing out of the ordinary, for such was to be expected in the name of war. He completely excused himself and failed to acknowledge that he was complicit in the murder of the woman's husband.

The passage takes up with Nathan, David's counselor, being sent by the Lord to force David to face the truth about who he had become. Nathan began by way of a parable. David took the story to be factual and became righteously indignant with the rich man who robbed the poor man of his prized ewe for his own pleasure. David even declared the man absent of pity and deserving of death!

Nathan's tale should have immediately provoked a hint of recognition to David's situation, but as obvious from his reaction, David remained clueless to Nathan's purpose—not at all seeing his role in the story. David did not want to see the truth about who he had really become because it made him look bad. The truth was that he was both an adulterer and a murderer. Until he confessed that truth, he would meet with God's displeasure and would be unable to achieve any of the things that God had in store for his future. But when Nathan made the point of his parable clear, David claimed the truth about himself. He acknowledged that he had committed a great sin. It was only after David embraced his complete persona—flaws and all—that God spoke a word of redemption into David's life.

From David's example, we learn the importance of being blatantly honest about who we are, even when it is unattractive or painful. If we allow ourselves to remain in denial about our faults and weaknesses, then we cannot seek God's help to improve them. Our flaws then become stumbling blocks that keep us from achieving our goals and becoming the persons that we should be according to the Lord's good purpose. However, when we openly expose ourselves before God, He will speak a message of redemption into our lives as He did for David, and we will be able to make positive transformations.

❖ THE WORD IN ACTION

1. We all at some point have received criticism, constructive or otherwise, from someone else. Recall when this may have occurred in your recent past. How did you respond? What do you think your response reveals about you?

   _____

   _____

   _____

   _____

   _____

2. As opposed to reacting defensively to criticism, what do you think is the best course of action?

   _____

   _____

   _____

   _____

   _____

3. How can you turn criticism into a positive opportunity for you to discover yourself?

   _____

   _____

   _____

   _____

   _____

CHAPTER 8

THE ABCs OF DISCOVERING OURSELVES

As we have discussed thus far, discovering our true identities—the persons that we are meant to be—is no easy task. The purpose of this chapter is to identify a systematic process to unveiling the persons that God wants us to be. The process follows three steps that we will call, *The ABCs of self-discovery:*

- **A—Acknowledge** who we are, including the flaws and weaknesses that do not meet God's approval.
- **B—Believe** that God is able to remove any hindrance that stands between who you are today and who you are to become.
- **C—Convert** by being determined in your mind to transform your life by whatever means necessary with the help of God.

The case study that we will use for this chapter centers on the apostle Peter. Peter was a zealous follower of Christ but he possessed some serious character flaws. Peter thought that he knew all there was to know about his character and identity. He was sure that he would be the most faithful of the Lord's disciples. But poor Peter had overlooked a few things. Only after following the *ABCs of self-discovery* was he able to become the man that he and the Lord wanted him to be.

❖ THE PASSAGE

John 21:15-19

15 When they had finished eating, Jesus said to Simon Peter, "Simon son of John, do you truly love me more than these?" "Yes, Lord," he said, "you know that I love you." Jesus said, "Feed my lambs."

16 Again Jesus said, "Simon son of John, do you truly love me?" He answered, "Yes, Lord, you know that I love you." Jesus said, "Take care of my sheep."

17 The third time he said to him, "Simon son of John, do you love me?" Peter was hurt because Jesus asked him the third time, "Do you love me?" He said, "Lord, you know all things; you know that I love you." Jesus said, "Feed my sheep.

18 I tell you the truth, when you were younger you dressed yourself and went where you wanted; but when you are old you will stretch out your hands, and someone else will dress you and lead you where you do not want to go."

19 Jesus said this to indicate the kind of death by which Peter would glorify God. Then he said to him, "Follow me!"

❖ THE STUDY

We often remember Peter as the outspoken, over-confident disciple of Jesus. Peter swore his loyalty to Jesus and even declared that he would stick by Jesus' side when all the other disciples scattered. Peter was sure of himself. Even when the Lord looked into Peter and saw his weakness, telling him how he would deny the Lord before the crowds, Peter in effect said, "No, not me, Lord. That's not who I am." However, we well recall what happened when Peter was questioned after Jesus' arrest: Peter denied any association with the Lord *three* times. Peter did not know himself as well as he thought he did.

However, on a later occasion, Jesus gave Peter the opportunity to rediscover himself. After Jesus was raised from the dead, He appeared to all of His apostles. Our passage for this chapter chronicles a conversation between Peter and Jesus. Jesus asked Peter whether he really loved Him; two times Peter answered in the affirmative. The Lord asked him a third time. At this third repetition, Peter felt remorse, but he inwardly *acknowledged* that his earlier denials had been a disappointment and had exhibited flaws in his character.

Next, Peter voiced his *belief* that the Lord knows and is in control of all things. With such faith, Peter could be sure that the Lord would help him overcome this character flaw in order to fulfill any assignment with which he would be entrusted. Last, Peter proved that he had *converted* by confirming his love for the Lord and accepting his invitation to follow Him.

As we follow Peter through the rest of the New Testament, we learn that he had truly discovered himself. With the help of the Lord, he faithfully served in the early church and boldly defended the Christian faith before those who opposed it up until his death.

Likewise, we can discover the persons that we were meant to be by following the *ABCs of self-discovery*:
- Acknowledge
- Believe
- Convert

❖ THE WORD IN ACTION

Two other men, both criminals, were also led out with him to be executed. When they came to the place called the Skull, there they crucified him, along with the criminals—one on his right, the other on his left. Jesus said, "Father, forgive them, for they do not know what they are doing." And they divided up his clothes by casting lots. The people stood watching, and the rulers even sneered at him. They said, "He saved others; let him save himself if he is the Christ of God, the Chosen One." The soldiers also came up and mocked him.

They offered him wine vinegar and said, "If you are the king of the Jews, save yourself." There was a written notice above him, which read: THIS IS THE KING OF THE JEWS. One of the criminals who hung there hurled insults at him: "Aren't you the Christ? Save yourself and us!" But the other criminal rebuked him. "Don't you fear God," he said, "since you are under the same sentence? We are punished justly, for we are getting what our deeds deserve. But this man has done nothing wrong." Then he said, "Jesus, remember me when you come into your kingdom." Jesus answered him, "I tell you the truth, today you will be with me in paradise."—Luke 23:32-43

1. From this passage, identify and explain the *ABCs of self-discovery* as it applies to the situation of the converted criminal.

   _____

   _____

   _____

   _____

   _____

2. How does this passage demonstrate that as long as we have life, we have hope for self-discovery and transformation?

   _____

   _____

   _____

   _____

   _____

3. How does Jesus' promise to the converted criminal affect you?

   _____

   _____

   _____

   _____

   _____

CHAPTER 9

THE JOURNEY (PART 1)— SPIRITUAL AUTOBIOGRAPHY

A key to discovering our true selves is to understand our personal story and how it has shaped our identities. Our collections of experiences have a phenomenal impact on the persons that we become. Even as our lives undergo transformation, we carry with us a personal history that, as we grow, we build upon and edify.

The purpose of this chapter is to help us to see the importance of composing our own spiritual autobiographies in order to better understand our unique identities. Our biblical case study is none other than Saul the Pharisee, who became Paul the apostle. In following Paul's journey through conversion, we will observe how his experiences affected the man that he would become.

❖ THE PASSAGE

Acts 9:1-19

1 Meanwhile, Saul was still breathing out murderous threats against the Lord's disciples. He went to the high priest

2 and asked him for letters to the synagogues in Damascus, so that if he found any there who belonged to the Way, whether men or women, he might take them as prisoners to Jerusalem.

3 As he neared Damascus on his journey, suddenly a light from heaven flashed around him.

4 He fell to the ground and heard a voice say to him, "Saul, Saul, why do you persecute me?"

5 "Who are you, Lord?" Saul asked. "I am Jesus, whom you are persecuting," he replied.

6 "Now get up and go into the city, and you will be told what you must do."

7 The men traveling with Saul stood there speechless; they heard the sound but did not see anyone.

8 Saul got up from the ground, but when he opened his eyes he could see nothing. So they led him by the hand into Damascus.

9 For three days he was blind, and did not eat or drink anything.

10 In Damascus there was a disciple named Ananias. The Lord called to him in a vision, "Ananias!" "Yes, Lord," he answered.

11 The Lord told him, "Go to the house of Judas on Straight Street and ask for a man from Tarsus named Saul, for he is praying.

12 In a vision he has seen a man named Ananias come and place his hands on him to restore his sight."

13 "Lord," Ananias answered, "I have heard many reports about this man and all the harm he has done to your saints in Jerusalem.

14 And he has come here with authority from the chief priests to arrest all who call on your name."

15 But the Lord said to Ananias, "Go! This man is my chosen instrument to carry my name before the Gentiles and their kings and before the people of Israel.

16 I will show him how much he must suffer for my name."

17 Then Ananias went to the house and entered it. Placing his hands on Saul, he said, "Brother Saul, the Lord—Jesus, who appeared to you on the road as you were coming here—has sent me so that you may see again and be filled with the Holy Spirit."

18 Immediately, something like scales fell from Saul's eyes, and he could see again. He got up and was baptized,

19 and after taking some food, he regained his strength. Saul spent several days with the disciples in Damascus.

❖ THE STUDY

This passage provides a snapshot into the biography of the apostle Paul. However, we will expand this into a panoramic view with the aid of other tidbits found throughout the New Testament writings.

We begin with Paul's early childhood. He was born to Jewish parents in the city of Tarsus, the capital of the Roman province of Cilicia. It was a commercially profitable city and was well known as a Greek cultural center. Having Jewish parents, young Saul would have attended a Jewish primary school. It is also likely that he learned his trade of tent making from his father while living at home.

Paul indicated that as an adolescent, he was educated in a rabbinic school, mentored by one of the famed teachers of that day—Gamaliel. He became well versed in the law and he was named foremost among his peers. In addition to his Jewish heritage and Greek influences, Saul was apparently also a Roman citizen, a status that was likely granted to or purchased by one of his ancestors. Consequently, Saul could claim a very prestigious pedigree.

Educated according to Jewish tradition, Saul developed an intense hatred toward the Lord's disciples. Having been taught that this was a sect of blasphemous miscreants, he along with other Jewish leaders sought to eradicate them. He engaged in gross forms of persecution against the early church. In fact, he was present at the trial of Stephen and condoned his death by stoning.

Saul was zealous in his persecution of the early Christians. Although his efforts were misdirected, Saul sincerely believed that he was in support of the worthier cause. As a result, Saul was not only satisfied in cleansing Jerusalem of those belonging to the sect called *The Way*, but also, he went above and beyond—getting approval from the Sanhedrin and high priest—to seek out those in Damascus who professed the name Jesus. It proved to be a road trip that Saul would never forget.

On the road to Damascus, the Lord (in all His glory) appeared from heaven and declared Himself to be Jesus. Can you imagine how dumbfounded Saul must have been? Only a short time prior, Stephen had declared a vision of the glorious Lord Jesus in heaven at God's right hand. But those present at the Sanhedrin, to include Saul, had not wanted to hear it. They subsequently stoned him for it. Saul then was blinded by the glory of the same one, Jesus.

Led into Damascus by those in company with him, Saul remained there, praying. Likely, this miraculous experience caused Saul to question everything that he had been taught by Jewish traditionalists and possibly even ponder over the person that he had become. Ananias arrived to reassure Saul that the events three days past were not a dream. The Lord had truly appeared to Saul and Ananias conveyed the Holy Spirit upon him. No longer blinded by ambition and tradition, Saul could *see* the Lord's purpose for his life. After his conversion, Saul continued to seek out souls belonging to The Way, but with renewed purpose. No longer did he seek to haze and eradicate, but to save and educate.

What can we learn from following Paul's biography? Just as we are better able to understand who Paul was by familiarizing ourselves with the intimate details of his life story, we will be in a better position to understand who we are as individuals by reacquainting ourselves with our own life story. We may not expect to uncover a blaring epiphany such as Paul experienced on the road to Damascus. However, if we are careful, we will uncover truths about ourselves that will reveal who we are in life and where we are meant to be.

❖ THE WORD IN ACTION

Reflect on your life's journey thus far. Think about the memories and experiences from (1) early childhood, (2) adolescence, and (3) adulthood that helped shape the person that you are today.

_____

_____

_____

_____

_____

_____

_____

_____

_____

_____

_____

_____

_____

_____

_____

_____

CHAPTER 10

THE JOURNEY (PART 2)—CONTEXT

The next phase of our journey to discovering ourselves is identifying our current context or the environment in which we have been placed. Before we can fully comprehend our role and be effective in our efforts to become children of God fit to do His purpose, we must clearly understand the ministry in which we have been placed. To be sure, our context may vary and require adaptation on our parts, but these adjustments should not alter our core identities as believers. Rather, as we interact with multiple contexts, our identities should be refined and become more comprehensive.

In following the apostle Paul's journey, we will observe how he applied the principle of identifying his context and using that knowledge to enable him to become a well-rounded minister of the Lord. Throughout the course of his ministerial career, Paul found himself in various contexts that differed greatly from one another. Paul employed the use of keen observation and research to gain a deeper understanding of his environment, as we will note in this chapter's biblical case study.

❖ THE PASSAGE

Acts 17:16-23

16 While Paul was waiting for them in Athens, he was greatly distressed to see that the city was full of idols.

17 So he reasoned in the synagogue with the Jews and the God-fearing Greeks, as well as in the marketplace day by day with those who happened to be there.

18 A group of Epicurean and Stoic philosophers began to dispute with him. Some of them asked, "What is this babbler trying to say?" Others remarked, "He seems to be advocating foreign gods." They said this because Paul was preaching the good news about Jesus and the resurrection.

19 Then they took him and brought him to a meeting of the Areopagus, where they said to him, "May we know what this new teaching is that you are presenting?

20 You are bringing some strange ideas to our ears, and we want to know what they mean."

21 (All the Athenians and the foreigners who lived there spent their time doing nothing but talking about and listening to the latest ideas.)

22 Paul then stood up in the meeting of the Areopagus and said: "Men of Athens! I see that in every way you are very religious.

23 For as I walked around and looked carefully at your objects of worship, I even found an altar with this inscription: TO AN UNKNOWN GOD. Now what you worship as something unknown I am going to proclaim to you.

❖ THE STUDY

While Paul was awaiting the arrival of his missionary companions, Silas and Timothy, he took note of his surroundings there in Athens. Known to be the center of Greek culture at that time, the city was full of temples, idols, and shrines dedicated to the pagan gods of the Grecian world. Although disturbed, Paul set about ministering to the Jews and other God-fearing Greeks in the city.

However, Paul did not limit his context to the synagogue. He realized that those pagan Greeks needed to hear the Gospel also. The challenge would be finding a way to minister in a context so conversely different from his custom. Not one to shy away from his God-given responsibility, Paul entered into the marketplace of Athens—where philosophers and intellectuals gathered.

An examination of his context revealed that Paul held the audience of two notable groups: the Epicureans and the Stoics. These were philosophers who advocated different ideas regarding the existence of a higher power. The Epicureans believed that gods exist, but they were not concerned with human affairs. Stoics contended that human souls were all a part of one obscure deity and that the eventuality of humans would be either universal destruction or reabsorption back into the deity. Although Paul's own faith conflicted with both these schools of ideas, knowledge of what each group believed would be helpful in how he adapted his message to them.

Paul also gained insight about his context by observing the surrounding environment. As mentioned earlier, the city was filled with temples and shrines. Paul did not just discard their appearance as repulsive dedications to pagan gods, but he took note of them and used the information he gathered to help him better understand his context.

Later, when he addressed the Athenians, Paul was able to use his background knowledge of the people assimilated with the information that he gathered walking through the city to effectively develop a speech that would capture their attention. Paul spoke of things that the people could understand and relate to. He communicated on a subject that held their interest. Yet, all the while, Paul remained true to his purpose and true to his identity as a believer and publisher of Christ.

From Paul's example, we can appreciate the importance of familiarizing ourselves with our context. Even when the context may seem almost foreign to the things and ideas that we are accustomed to, by being observant and educating ourselves, we will uncover helpful tidbits that will enable us to be more effective in our ministry. Like Paul, we may find it necessary to adapt our approach, but never do we compromise our faith as believers. Our goal is to seek an inroad into our context and follow it while remaining true to our purpose and identity as believers and children of God.

❖ THE WORD IN ACTION

List and describe the current contexts with which you interact on a regular basis (at least once a week).

_____

_____

_____

_____

_____

_____

_____

_____

_____

_____

_____

_____

_____

_____

_____

_____

CHAPTER **11**

THE JOURNEY (PART 3)—SYNERGY

We should recognize that God brings us to places and circumstances for a purpose. Sometimes that purpose is not always conspicuous, but with meditation and prayer we appreciate that in whatever position we find ourselves we are given the opportunity to positively affect our context as well as gain new insights into our own personas. The symbiotic relationship that exists between our lives and our contexts can also be termed as *synergy*.

Synergy can be achieved once we have carefully reviewed our journey thus far (spiritual autobiography) and judiciously observed our context (contextual analysis). Once we have a clear understanding of ourselves (who we are, how we got here, and where we are going), and our context—its strengths, weaknesses, spiritual background, and intellectual makeup—then we can begin to see where these two subjects intersect. It becomes clearer to us how God is using our current position to improve us and minister to our context.

Continuing with Paul's ministry, we note that God placed Paul in many different contexts and as he adapted to the various settings, Paul became a better minister, and the purpose of the Lord was accomplished in founding the early churches. Both Paul and the context were mutually benefited.

❖ THE PASSAGE

1 Corinthians 15:1-11

1 Now, brothers, I want to remind you of the gospel I preached to you, which you received and on which you have taken your stand.

2 By this gospel you are saved, if you hold firmly to the word I preached to you. Otherwise, you have believed in vain.

3 For what I received I passed on to you as of first importance: that Christ died for our sins according to the Scriptures,

4 that he was buried, that he was raised on the third day according to the Scriptures,

5 and that he appeared to Peter, and then to the Twelve.

6 After that, he appeared to more than five hundred of the brothers at the same time, most of whom are still living, though some have fallen asleep.

7 Then he appeared to James, then to all the apostles,

8 and last of all he appeared to me also, as to one abnormally born.

9 For I am the least of the apostles and do not even deserve to be called an apostle, because I persecuted the church of God.

10 But by the grace of God I am what I am, and his grace to me was not without effect. No, I worked harder than all of them—yet not I, but the grace of God that was with me.

11 Whether, then, it was I or they, this is what we preach, and this is what you believed.

❖ THE STUDY

This passage is taken from a letter that the apostle Paul wrote to the early church in Corinth. Years earlier, Paul had actually ministered in Corinth and he was instrumental in establishing the Christian church there. At that time, Paul was merely responding to the assignment given to him by the Lord to go and minister to the nations. However, Paul would later discover that his own personal experience merged with the state of the Corinthian church in an interesting way.

After Paul left the church in Corinth to continue his missionary travels, Grecian influences began to seep into the church. Some of the Jews and Greeks there who were once believers began to declare that there was no resurrection. When this news reached the apostle Paul, he was no doubt stricken that persons whom he considered to be his children had followed such blasphemous teachings.

He then sought to appeal to their sense of logic by reminding them of how he first preached the Gospel to them and the faith that they showed. He repeated the message on which salvation is based: Christ died for our sins. However, Paul's argument gained force when he added the physical proof of the Resurrection.

Many had seen the resurrected Christ before He ascended to heaven. But Paul was able to offer personal confirmation to the Corinthian church. While yet a persecutor of Christians, the resurrected Lord Jesus appeared to him to give him commission. Paul not only had a testimony to prove that Jesus had been resurrected, but Paul had a testimony of God's beautiful grace. He was able to preach God's grace to the Corinthian church because he had received it, lived in it, and thrived by it. All the other apostles had likewise seen the resurrected Christ and like all of us, received God's grace. But few had the testimony that Paul had, and it was that testimony that the Corinthians needed to put them back on track.

Paul also benefitted from his interaction with his context. He honed his skills as a minister as he defended the Christian faith to them.

He deepened his own personal conviction toward his hope and salvation. And though the Corinthian church had its flaws, it also had rewarding strengths. In his letters, Paul spoke of the joy he received in hearing about their progress. When he was personally experiencing persecution and bondage, the church of Corinth remained vigilant in their prayers for him and sent comforting words to him to keep him encouraged and strong.

So, then, in considering this biblical case study, we can appreciate that God placed Paul in his context for a divine purpose that mutually benefited both. It is the same for us today: the Lord puts us in a position for a purpose. Whatever circumstance we may find ourselves in, we are exactly where we need to be in our journey. It may be challenging and difficult to understand at first, but if we faithfully pursue it, then we will likely uncover what God has in store for us in our current context.

Like Paul, we all have a story. God has given us our stories and placed us where we need to be. However, it is up to us to find the connection and make it work. If we accept the challenge, then we will be on our way to truly discovering ourselves and realizing our full potential.

❖ THE WORD IN ACTION

1. Comparing your notes from chapters 9 and 10, in what way do you feel that you connect to your contexts?

    _____

    _____

    _____

    _____

    _____

    _____

2. What positive value do you bring to your context?

_____

_____

_____

_____

_____

_____

3. How does your context contribute to your personal self-discovery?

_____

_____

_____

_____

_____

_____

CHAPTER 12

"WHO AM I?"

In the process of discovering ourselves, we may have uncovered some of our hidden assets and untapped strengths. We may have also found a few skeletons and traits that we are not as proud of. Still, we are who we are. We can work to grow and improve ourselves, but we must remember that as believers we are ultimately God's children, despite our flaws. The Lord sees us as we are and He loves us still.

King David penned a heart-stirring psalm to express his appreciation for the unique identity he possessed and the relationship that he shared with the Lord. By reflecting on this psalm, we are reminded that despite our faults, we are beautiful in the eyes of God.

❖ THE PASSAGE

Psalm 139:1-24

1 O L<small>ORD</small>, you have searched me and you know me.

2 You know when I sit and when I rise; you perceive my thoughts from afar.

3 You discern my going out and my lying down; you are familiar with all my ways.

4 Before a word is on my tongue you know it completely, O L<small>ORD</small>.

5 You hem me in—behind and before; you have laid your hand upon me.

6 Such knowledge is too wonderful for me, too lofty for me to attain.

7 Where can I go from your Spirit? Where can I flee from your presence?

8 If I go up to the heavens, you are there; if I make my bed in the depths, you are there.

9 If I rise on the wings of the dawn, if I settle on the far side of the sea,

10 even there your hand will guide me, your right hand will hold me fast.

11 If I say, "Surely the darkness will hide me and the light becomes night around me,"

12 even the darkness will not be dark to you; the night will shine like the day, for darkness is as light to you.

13 For you created my inmost being; you knit me together in my mother's womb.

14 I praise you because I am fearfully and wonderfully made; your works are wonderful, I know that full well.

15 My frame was not hidden from you when I was

made in the secret place. When I was woven together in the depths of the earth,

16 your eyes saw my unformed body. All the days ordained for me were written in your book before one of them came to be.

17 How precious to me are your thoughts, O God! How vast is the sum of them!

18 Were I to count them, they would outnumber the grains of sand. When I awake, I am still with you.

19 If only you would slay the wicked, O God! Away from me, you bloodthirsty men!

20 They speak of you with evil intent; your adversaries misuse your name.

21 Do I not hate those who hate you, O LORD, and abhor those who rise up against you?

22 I have nothing but hatred for them; I count them my enemies.

23 Search me, O God, and know my heart; test me and know my anxious thoughts.

24 See if there is any offensive way in me, and lead me in the way everlasting.

❖ THE STUDY

In this psalm, David asked the Lord to search him—to look into his heart—and see who he really was. If we seek to discover our true identities, then we have only to request the same of the Lord and He will reveal it to us. David said that the Lord searched him and was able to know him, his thoughts, and all his ways. Because of God's intimate knowledge of him, David was confident that the Lord was ever present in his life. Similarly, when we choose to open ourselves up to the Lord's scrutiny, we enter into a personal relationship with Him. He has us in His loving care. Even with all of our blunders and faults, God is with us. We have the assurance from David's psalm that there is nowhere that we can run, nowhere that we could hide, that would be beyond the reach of the Lord and the Holy Spirit. Whatever wrongs we have done, whatever character traits cause us to fall down, God promises not to leave us, as long as we do not leave Him.

David inquired that the Lord see if there existed in David's persona *any offensive way.* In other words, David asked the Lord, "Find what's wrong and help me to fix it." We should have the same attitude. Our goal as believers is to become persons fit to reflect God's glory. Therefore, we should welcome God's critical evaluation and then work to bring our lives in harmony with His standards. We have God's promise that He will not only help us, but if we conform to His purpose, He will also "lead [us] in the way everlasting."

David also reminds us of a very important fact that should be a prominent part of our personal self-awareness: each individual is wonderfully made. Therefore, we should not be overly discouraged by our weaknesses. We should not become obsessed in comparing ourselves with others. We should not allow others to place unrealistic expectations on our lives. The Lord created each and every one of us as a unique person. Before the Lord rested from His creative works, He looked at the things He had created, including humans, and declared that everything was very good. David echoed the sentiment by stating, "Your works are wonderful." So regardless of where we are in the process of refining ourselves, we should be proud of who we are—we are children of God. We celebrate our existence and we praise our Lord because we are fearfully and wonderfully made.

❖ THE WORD IN ACTION

This then is how we know that we belong to the truth, and how we set our hearts at rest in his presence whenever our hearts condemn us. For God is greater than our hearts, and he knows everything. Dear friends, if our hearts do not condemn us, we have confidence before God and receive from him anything we ask, because we obey his commands and do what pleases him. And this is his command: to believe in the name of his Son, Jesus Christ, and to love one another as he commanded us.—1 John 3:19-23

1. How can our hearts condemn us?

   _____
   _____
   _____
   _____
   _____

2. What does it mean to you that "God is greater than our hearts"?

   _____
   _____
   _____
   _____
   _____

3. Do you find it reassuring that God knows *everything* about you? Why or why not?

   _____
   _____
   _____
   _____
   _____

4. Why is it important to celebrate who we are even though we are admittedly flawed?

   _____
   _____
   _____
   _____
   _____

CPSIA information can be obtained
at www.ICGtesting.com
Printed in the USA
BVHW060227141222
654203BV00014B/547